HOW TO ASK GREAT QUESTIONS

HOW TO
ASK GREAT
QUESTIONS

GUIDE DISCUSSION
BUILD RELATIONSHIPS
DEEPEN FAITH

KAREN LEE-THORP

A NavPress resource published in alliance
with Tyndale House Publishers, Inc.

NavPress is the publishing ministry of The Navigators, an international Christian organization and leader in personal spiritual development. NavPress is committed to helping people grow spiritually and enjoy lives of meaning and hope through personal and group resources that are biblically rooted, culturally relevant, and highly practical.

For more information, visit www.NavPress.com.

How to Ask Great Questions: Guide Discussion, Build Relationships, Deepen Faith

A NavPress resource published in alliance with Tyndale House Publishers, Inc.

NAVPRESS is a registered trademark of NavPress, The Navigators, Colorado Springs, CO. The NAVPRESS logo is a trademark of NavPress, The Navigators. *TYNDALE* is a registered trademark of Tyndale House Publishers, Inc. Absence of ® in connection with marks of NavPress or other parties does not indicate an absence of those marks.

The Team:
Don Pape, Publisher
David Zimmerman, Editor
Elizabeth Symm, Copy Editor
Jennifer Ghionzoli, Designer

Some of the anecdotal illustrations in this book are true to life and are included with the permission of the persons involved. All other illustrations are composites of real situations, and any resemblance to people living or dead is purely coincidental.

For information about special discounts for bulk purchases, please contact Tyndale House Publishers at csresponse@tyndale.com, or call 1-800-323-9400.

Cataloging-in-Publication Data is available.

ISBN 978-1-64158-132-5

Printed in the United States of America

24	23	22	21	20	19	18
7	6	5	4	3	2	1

CONTENTS

1

WHAT THIS BOOK IS ABOUT

The Power of a Good Question

Once when Jesus was praying in private and his disciples were with him, he asked them, "Who do the crowds say I am?"

They replied, "Some say John the Baptist; others say Elijah; and still others, that one of the prophets of long ago has come back to life."

"But what about you?" he asked. "Who do you say I am?"

Peter answered, "God's Messiah."

LUKE 9:18-20

JESUS WAS A BRILLIANT TEACHER. He knew how to tell a story that would propel people into thinking in new categories. He was king of the one-liner. And He understood the power of a well-timed, well-phrased question.

- "Who do the crowds say I am?" (Luke 9:18)
- "Do you want to get well?" (John 5:6)
- "What do you think about the Messiah? Whose son is he?" (Matthew 22:42)
- "What do you want me to do for you?" (Luke 18:41)
- "Which of the two did what his father wanted?" (Matthew 21:31)

Jesus' questions were simple, clear, never condescending, always provocative. They made people think for themselves and examine their hearts. Jesus' questions were always fresh and attuned to the unique needs of the people He was talking to. Instead of following a rote method, He seems to have thought about how His questions would affect His audience.

Research tells us that people remember far more of what they say than what they hear, and far more of what they discover for themselves than what they are spoon-fed. Hence, a question that sparks discovery and gets people to say out loud what they know is an essential tool in teaching. And in a small group, the question is everything.

This book will equip you to ask questions that

- build relationships between people
- help people analyze a passage of the Bible or another book
- draw out opinions and feelings
- follow up on a primary question
- guide people in applying the Bible to their unique lives
- guide a group in solving a problem or reaching a decision

You will find this book useful if you

- lead a small group
- teach Sunday school
- teach in any interactive learning environment
- chair a group or committee that makes decisions

The table of contents is annotated so you can investigate just the topic you are looking for, or you can read cover to cover. Some sections will refer you to other sections for more on a related topic.

KAREN'S TOP TEN PRINCIPLES FOR ASKING GREAT QUESTIONS

First, a few general principles.

1. This is a discussion, not a test.

A test is a situation in which the person asking the questions knows all the right answers, and the responder's task is to give the right answers. Test questions are fine in high-school algebra class or in the oral exam for a doctoral candidate. Test questions are useful when your goal is to see if people can parrot back information they have memorized, such as in a foreign-language class. However, when either spiritual growth or sharing among peers is a goal of your group, test questions can cause problems.

For one thing, tests tend to put people on the defensive—they worry about giving the wrong answer and appearing foolish, so their pulse rises and adrenaline flows. Adrenaline is good for those running marathons, but it hinders creative thinking. In fact, it actually floods out those portions of the brain in which people do creative thinking.

By contrast, a relaxed but stimulating environment, one in which people feel welcomed and engaged, is the kind most likely to encourage people to consider new ideas, examine their lives, and entertain the possibility of changing their behavior.

Second, tests imply a hierarchy. The teacher has the right answers and so is superior to the students. In a class on prayer, it may be true that the teacher knows more about prayer than the students do. The teacher may impart some of his or her knowledge to the students. But when the teacher asks a question about prayer, it needs to be very clear in everyone's mind whether the teacher wants the class to think for themselves or repeat something the teacher has said. A test question is okay if everyone understands they are reviewing material they have heard before, but when a test question is disguised as a discussion question, people feel put down. A group designed for spiritual growth requires shared power and an atmosphere of mutual respect. Test questions disguised as discussion questions don't feel respectful.

As a rule of thumb, discussion questions usually look for information members of the group have but the leader may not have:

- What do you think? (Only you know what you think.)
- What feelings does Jesus' statement provoke in you?
- With which character do you most identify in this passage?
- What contrasts do you notice in this story?

In all of these cases, the person asking the question is looking for something he or she genuinely doesn't know. That's how questions work in normal conversation.

However, when the task at hand involves drawing out the facts of a text, there are some important questions to be asked that have right-or-wrong answers:

- Who are the primary characters in this story?
- How did the jailer respond after the earthquake in Acts 16?

Because fact-finding or observation questions tend to have right answers, and because the person asking the question has usually spent more time examining the text than the responders have, it's easy for such questions to make a discussion feel like a test. Chapter 3 will address how to ask observation questions in a way that minimizes the test feeling, avoids boring the group, and yet draws out the essential facts.

What does a disguised test question look like? It may ask for mind reading:

What five key features of the sanctified mind does Paul describe in Romans 8?

Since Paul doesn't list five principles in any obvious way in Romans 8, this question asks responders to read the questioner's mind. The group leader has identified five principles in the chapter, and the group's job is to figure out what they are. In chapter 3, we'll discuss the difference between asking people to observe what the text says and asking them to read your mind.

Alternatively, a test question may ask people for information not currently available to them:

What does Paul mean by the term *flesh* in Ephesians 2:3?

Flesh is a somewhat technical term in Paul's vocabulary. Scholars have a lively debate running between at least two points of view. It would be helpful to explain this word in a few clear sentences to your group, but unless you know your group has heard this information before, it's probably unwise to ask them to supply it. You're likely to be met with embarrassed silence and have to answer the question yourself. You have then asked a rhetorical question, not fostered a discussion.

Chances are that if you do this often enough, people will begin to assume that all of your questions are rhetorical and will stop trying to answer them.

Even worse, a test question may ask people to defend themselves:

> Q: What do you think Paul means by saying we were dead in our sins?
> A: I think he means . . .
> Q: Why do you say that?

"What do you think" is a perfectly respectable way to ask a question. It asks for information that the responder has and the questioner does not have. However, "Why?" as a follow-up question can make people fear you think their answer was defective. In chapter 6, we'll explore ways of probing for more information without placing people on the defensive.

2. Avoid leading the witness.

If you've watched much TV courtroom drama, you know that attorneys often lead witnesses because it is to the interrogator's advantage to make the witness say what he wants the jury to hear. You also know that leading the witness usually causes the opposing attorney to object.

A small-group leader or classroom teacher may want the group to get at some information she thinks is important. But being committed to a question-and-answer format, she may ask something like

- Don't you think that not taking the Lord's name in vain includes being careful about saying, "God told me"?
- In what ways are you like the Pharisees in this passage?
- Does this passage make you feel angry or glad?

Each of these questions puts words into the responders' mouths. "Don't you think" is a manipulative way of telling people what to think. There's nothing wrong with a leader saying what he thinks, as long as he takes responsibility for those thoughts: "*I think* that not taking the Lord's name in vain includes . . ." "Don't you think" introduces a teaching point or opinion disguised as a question.

The second question assumes that everybody in the group resembles the Pharisees. Perhaps it's true that we're all hypocritical or greedy or cowardly to some degree, but most of us prefer to confess our own sins rather than having others do it for us. This question has the feel of "When did you stop beating your wife?"

The third question offers an either/or alternative. It assumes there are only two possible responses to the passage. Anyone who finds the passage unnerving or sad or perhaps partly encouraging and partly threatening is out of luck. Either/or questions usually lead the witness.

3. Ask one question at a time.

How does the lack of forgiveness affect the one who has done harm, the one who has been harmed, and each person's relationship with God?

If you read that question a couple of times, you could probably take it apart and answer it piece by piece. But if you only heard it, you'd have forgotten the first part by the time you heard the last. It's best to ask just one simple question and wait for responses before asking the next piece:

- How does the lack of forgiveness affect the one who has done harm?
- How does it affect the one who has been harmed?

And so on. This principle is actually a subset of a larger one:

4. Make your questions accessible to everyone.

Keep questions simple enough that everybody has a reasonable chance of knowing what you mean the first time you say it. In addition to multiple questions like the one above, this principle weeds out questions with several linked clauses:

> Since eating meat sacrificed to idols might be confusing to a person who doesn't know the idols are nothing, and since eating meat in temples might inadvertently involve one in idolatrous worship, what is Paul's advice to the strong Christians in 1 Corinthians 8 regarding meat?

Technical terms can also leave people in the dust:

> In 1 Corinthians 7, how does Paul apply an eschatological hermeneutic to our process of decision-making about relationships?

I routinely scan my questions for words like *paradigm* whose meaning most people don't quite know but think they should.

Jesus' questions were always simple. Even so, nobody ever felt He was asking a question that was beneath his or her intelligence. Keeping the cookies where people can reach them doesn't require us to talk down to them. The simplest questions are usually the most profound.

5. Say what you mean.

It's easier to say what you mean when you keep a question simple. Still, it's often a good idea to go back over a list of questions and ask yourself, "Is this what I mean to ask?"

> What does it mean to the way we live that human beings are members of the family of God?

That's not a terrible question, but maybe what I really want to ask is "How do you think being members of God's family should affect the way we live?" That seems clearer.

> What does Pilate say when Jesus starts talking about truth?

It's okay to ask someone to quote the text before I ask them what the statement means. But perhaps it will be more economical for *me* to observe what Pilate says and ask *the group* what he means:

> When Pilate says, "What is truth?" what do you think he's asking Jesus? How would you put his question in your own words?

9

I'm always on the lookout for vagueness:

> How do you respond to what Jesus says in Matthew
> 5:17-20?

This question is likely to leave people wondering what kind of response I'm asking about. An emotional response? An opinion about the truth or falsehood of Jesus' statement? A personal application? I should specify

> What feelings does Jesus' statement in Matthew 5:17-20
> evoke in you?

Or

> In what ways is this paragraph relevant to us since we
> do not live under the Jewish law?

6. Take the direct route.

Again, simplicity rules. When formulating your question, be on the lookout for common detours like unnecessary clauses, irrelevant background, and double negatives.

> Why does it not make sense to not rely on the Spirit of
> God rather than on the flesh?

really means

> Why does Paul think it makes more sense to rely on
> the Spirit than on the flesh?

7. Ask open-ended questions.

> Q: Do you identify with the disciples in this passage?
> A: Not really.

"No" and "Yes" are not great conversation starters. A person can answer yes or no without even engaging his brain. By contrast, an open-ended question compels people to be attentive to the facts of a text or situation or to think carefully about the meaning of the facts.

There's nearly always a way to change a yes-or-no question into the question you really mean to ask:

> In what ways, if any, do you identify with the disciples here?

Without assuming that everyone must identify with the disciples, this question asks what we really want to know: not just whether, but how group members identify with the story. Notice that "In what ways" is even more open-ended than "In what way" because the latter assumes people can't identify in several ways.

> Are there seven key words in this paragraph?

This question both leads the witness and asks for merely a yes-or-no answer. What we mean is

> What key words do you notice in this paragraph?

Fact-finding questions become boring when they are closed-ended, asking for a single word or short phrase:

According to Genesis 1:1, who created the heavens and the earth?

Chapter 3 will explore ways of keeping fact questions from insulting the group.

8. Help people talk to each other.

It's easy for a guided discussion to focus on the leader. The leader asks a question, and one person answers. The leader asks another question, and another person answers. Everyone looks at the leader and talks to the leader.

In a healthy group, people talk to each other. The leader asks a question, someone responds, and someone else responds to what the previous person said. They look at each other. If people are not automatically talking to each other, there are ways to encourage them to do so. Chapter 5 will address follow-up questions that help people respond to one another. Chapter 2 will explain how getting people to tell their stories builds the kinds of relationships that undergird genuine discussions.

9. Pay attention to details.

Some people like to leap immediately into discussing what a passage of the Bible or a chapter of a book means to them personally without examining what it says. Such discussions can quickly lose sight of the topic or passage you're studying. By zeroing in on the details—characters, events, setting, key words, and phrases—we see things in a text that may alter our preconceptions. Chapter 3 will equip you to help a group dig out the details.

Incidentally, some people are detail people. They enjoy wading into the minutiae, and they do it well. When you spot people with this gift, recognize them for it. You can assign them the task of laying out the key details for the group and then thank them for their contribution. With any luck, others in the group will begin to appreciate the value of details and will also begin to ask themselves the important question "What gifts do I bring to this group?"

10. Don't lose sight of the big picture.

On the other hand, some people are good at seeing the big picture. Since the forest is as important as the trees, encourage those in your group who are good at

- summarizing what a paragraph, a chapter, a story, or a psalm is about
- understanding the original historical context of a passage and explaining it clearly
- seeing the similarities between our modern world and the ancient world addressed in the text
- keeping the group focused on its goals

Chapter 6 will address when and how to ask for a summary or check for a consensus about a decision. Chapter 7 will discuss how these other big-picture issues contribute to effective application of learning to life. Also included in chapter 7 is a general outline of how all the types and techniques explored in this book can work together during a typical small-group meeting.

But first, chapter 2 will unpack a principle so important

that it could easily rank with these top ten: build relationships. Without an increasingly solid foundation of trust, no group discussion can build very high. And questions are an essential component in the process of laying that foundation.

2

TELLING OUR STORIES

Sharing Questions

Who was God to you when you were a child?

What has been one of the best compliments you have received as an adult?

What does Easter mean to you personally?

Ten years from now, what are three words that you hope people will be able to use to describe you?

THESE ARE STORYTELLING QUESTIONS—ones that ask people to tell the stories of their past, their present, and their future.

WHY TELL STORIES?

Building Trust

Every group has work to do, whether it's studying a book, planning an inner-city tutoring program, or caring for members who have lost loved ones. Because there's so much to do and so little time, it's tempting to get right down to business. However, your business time will be far more productive if you first invest in building relationships among group members.

Any group work requires cooperation, and cooperation requires trust. Even people of goodwill don't walk into a group automatically trusting the other members enough to cooperate at their peak level. Trust has to be built board by board, like the frame of a house. You can frame a house quickly, but if you're not careful, it may collapse when a heavy upper level and roof are added.

For example, let's say your group's current goal is to learn what the book of Romans says and how its message is relevant to your lives. You can have a good, intellectual conversation about the first chapter of Romans, identifying the theme of the book and analyzing the main points of Paul's introductory rhetoric. But if you want to get personal—discussing questions like "What does it look like for a modern person to serve created things rather than the Creator? In what areas, if any, are you tempted to do that?"—you will need to know that you can trust the others in your group. Questions that move people forward in their spiritual journeys are often risky. It's hard enough to confront such issues personally, let alone in the company of others. The riskier the group's work is, the stronger the relationships will need to be.

Again, let's say your group is planning your church's next two years of short-term mission projects. You want an open and honest exploration of all the possibilities, and you also want to reach consensus without killing each other or spending every weeknight together for a month. A foundation of trust will be invaluable.

Trust develops as people get to know each other. When people come to a new group, they inwardly ask themselves questions:

- Do I fit here?
- Will I be able to do the work I have come to do?
- Do I like these people?
- Do they like me?
- Do we have anything in common, or do we come from opposite corners of the universe?
- Will they understand me?

People don't accomplish much work in a group until they get satisfactory answers to these questions. At best, a few people will barrel ahead while the others hang back because they don't feel safe. The full resources of the group will not become available until all members believe it is safe to offer themselves.

Telling stories is the easiest, fastest, safest way to help people get their trust questions answered. Storytelling questions are the easiest way to help people tell their stories. They make people feel welcome by inviting them to say, "This is who I am." The hearers, in turn, say to themselves, *Now that I know who you are, I see that we are both human, with commonalities and areas of uniqueness.*

Giving Care

Besides building trust, storytelling questions help people feel cared for. In many committee meetings, members work hard on tasks week after week with little sense that they or their contributions are valued. They may be struggling at work or home and may be longing for someone with whom to share their sadness or frustration. If the meeting provides no opportunity for personal sharing, some members will leave even more sad than they came; that way lies burnout. Others may make unnecessary speeches on the topic at hand in order to get attention; that is how meetings drag on for hours. Others may let out their frustration by sparking unproductive conflict.

By contrast, a single sharing question at the beginning of a meeting can drain off those negative emotions and nurture people with a feeling of care that leaves them energized for the group's business.

In a group whose purpose is spiritual growth, care is even more important. A growth group is in part a lab in which to practice the "one anothers" of Scripture: love one another, encourage one another, accept one another, pray for one another, and so on. Asking people who they are is a way of loving and accepting them. Hearing their answers lets us know how to encourage and pray for them.

PRINCIPLES OF STORYTELLING QUESTIONS

Dr. Roberta Hestenes defines "sharing questions" as "one-sentence questions that give people permission to be personal and talk about themselves without violating their dignity or requiring inappropriate self-disclosure."[1] One sentence is enough for simplicity. Talking about oneself means telling a piece of one's story. "Permission" and "without violating their dignity" imply that we have thought carefully about the level of self-disclosure that is appropriate for the group at hand.

How Long a Story?

A good storytelling question should invite at least one sentence in response. If you think the question "Where did you grow up?" will elicit only a city and state from your quiet group, ask for something that requires more of an answer:

Tell us one interesting fact about the town you grew up in.

On the other hand, under most circumstances, you don't want a question that will take each person five minutes to answer. If you have eight people, you have just used forty minutes for one question. You can help to assure that people will restrict their answers to under a minute if you answer first. Others will model the length of their answers on the time it takes you to tell your story.

There are times in a group's life when a ten- or even twenty-minute story is appropriate. You may want to set aside several meetings during which each person can tell his or her spiritual autobiography. This is the story of how a person found her way to God and what her journey with God has been like over the years. People learn an enormous amount about themselves by having to put this story together in a twenty-minute narrative. When the group has a chance to respond to what they've heard, the feedback is valuable for everyone, and the group bonds closely.[2]

How Revealing a Story?

Storytelling questions follow a progression from less vulnerable to more vulnerable. The icebreaker question you use to begin your third meeting together should require far less self-disclosure than the question you ask in the prayer time of a group that has been close for three years. If you answer the question first, you will model the level of vulnerability you are looking for. Generally, your answer should be just slightly more vulnerable than the responses you want from others.

For example, let's say you are going to be studying spiritual gifts and your opening question is

What is one thing you're good at?

If your answer is "cooking," you will probably get a series of single-phrase, not-very-vulnerable answers from the rest of your group. That's fine if people aren't ready to open up very much. If your answer is "I was the Student Activities chairperson at college, so I can throw a party for three hundred people," people may smile and loosen up a bit in their answers. If you say, "I am good at listening compassionately to people in pain because I've had a lot of pain in my life and I know how it feels," you'll set an entirely different tone. This is a serious, self-reflective, and bittersweet answer that will work only if your group is really ready to get down to business.

Past-Present-Future

The safest stories for most people to tell are about the past. Telling what we thought about God when we were ten is less vulnerable than telling what we think about God today. Also, talking about where we've been gives a group valuable perspective on where we are now. For these reasons, new groups often begin with sharing questions about the past.

For instance, if the group is going to explore the touchy topic of racism, two opening questions might be about childhood:

- Where did you grow up?
- What did you learn about other ethnic groups when you were a child?

This background will help the rest of the group understand why each person thinks the way he does in the present. It will lay a foundation for more vulnerable, recent-past questions such as

Describe a positive interaction you have had with a member of another ethnic group in the past year.

and the quite vulnerable present question

How do you think racial divisions affect your life today?

Future-oriented questions build on the past and present, so they are most useful when a group has been together for several sessions and is ready to begin revealing their hopes and dreams together:

How would you like your cross-cultural relationships to be different a year from now?

As a general rule, groups begin with questions about the past, move toward the present, and talk about the future when they've begun to know each other. However, plenty of present-day questions are basic enough for new groups:

- What do you do on a typical Wednesday?
- What do you like about your job?

And some future-oriented questions are fun icebreakers:

- If you inherited ten thousand dollars, what would you do with it?

Conversely, some past-oriented questions can lead your group into a minefield if any members of your group had traumatic childhoods. Don't ask, "What was your mother like?" unless you're prepared for people to unload or shut down.

Everyone Can Answer

It's important to design storytelling questions that everyone in the group can answer. Otherwise, some participants will feel excluded and embarrassed that their experience isn't "normal." For example, the question "What was your father like when you were growing up?" might easily exclude some people. If the subject of fatherhood is important to your group's task, you might word the question more broadly:

What emotions or images come to your mind when you think of the word *father*?

In the same way, unless you know the ages and backgrounds of your group members, it's wise not to assume that everyone in the group grew up with a Christian heritage or that everyone is old enough to remember landmark events. "How did you meet your spouse?" is fine if everyone in the group is married. Full-time family raisers may not mind "What do you like about your job?" but they may prefer "What do you like about the work you do?"

Positive versus Negative

A question that asks for positive information is almost always safer than one that invites negative information. For instance,

> Describe a positive interaction you have had with a member of another ethnic group in the past year.

will elicit positive stories that will tend to draw people together and make them feel good. The converse question,

> If you have had a negative interaction with a member of another ethnic group in the past year, please tell us about it.

invites people to get down to the nitty-gritty. The request may be important to ask at some point if you are going to get anywhere with the group's business, but it requires that a solid foundation of trust has already been laid. Sharing our positive stories gives us the courage to look together at life's unpleasant side. For this reason, a warm-up question at the beginning of a group session should normally aim for positive stories. The tougher negative stories can come later.

The exception to this rule is when you make a negative question an invitation for laughter:

> What is one of the worst vacation experiences you can recall?

Laughing over miserable or embarrassing experiences common to everyone—the worst date, worst job, or worst schoolteacher—is a great way to draw people together. Just be sure you've chosen a subject that people will likely laugh about.

The Best and the Worst

I often hear storytelling questions stated in extremes:

- What is the best . . .
- What is the worst . . .
- What was the biggest . . .
- What was the most embarrassing . . .

Questions stated in this way work fine for most people, but a few scrupulous people get stuck trying to choose which of their many embarrassing dates was truly the *most* embarrassing. And it doesn't matter. You're not really interested in precision here; you just want *any* story that fits the bill. To avoid frustrating this type of person, I usually ask for *one of* the best, worst, biggest, or most embarrassing date/job/school stories people can tell.

Related to the Task

Some people seem naturally wired to focus on tasks, and they approach relationships in a task-oriented way. Other people focus more on relationships, and getting tasks done is secondary. People can fall at one extreme or another on the task-relationship continuum, or they can fall somewhere in between.

Task-oriented people tend to gravitate toward committees.

Left to themselves, their relational lives can be impoverished. Relationship-oriented people tend to prefer supportive sharing groups, but left to themselves, they may get nothing done for anyone outside their circle. An effective community will draw on the strengths of each type of person so that people are cared for while a mission is being fulfilled.

Task-oriented people may find storytelling questions annoying unless they are linked to the task at hand. Relational people like to talk about themselves and hear others' stories just for the sake of getting to know each other, but task people like to feel they are accomplishing something. If you want task people to commit to your group, look for questions that relate to your immediate goal or larger mission. For instance, if you're going to study worship or plan a worship service, stories about good past experiences of worship are relevant. If you are studying workplace ethics, job-related stories make sense. If you are about to pray together, a reasonable question is

> What is one challenging situation you are currently facing?

If you are going to study Romans 3, you might ask,

> When you were a child, how did you typically respond when you got caught doing something wrong?

Good questions for committees include

- What excites you about being a part of this ministry?
- What obstacles could hinder you from accomplishing your goals for this team?

Know Your Group

In crafting storytelling questions, the most basic rule of thumb is simply to know your group. One group I know views both time and relationships as valuable commodities, so they hate wasting their time together with superficial questions. Even the newest members of that group have no trouble with a question like "How was conflict handled in your home when you were a child?"

For other groups, conflict is a threatening topic. They would need to know each other pretty well before they would tackle it. You are the expert on your group.

The storytelling question draws the group members together and gets them focused on something relevant to the group's agenda. It serves as a launching pad for the work of the group, whether that is studying a passage of the Bible or performing some tasks. If yours is a task group, you might turn next to chapter 8, which contains an approach to making effective decisions together. If yours is a study group, chapters 3 through 7 will outline a process for studying a text. Bible study is the emphasis in these chapters, but you'll find you can easily adapt this method for studying other books and materials.

3

JUST THE FACTS

Observation Questions

Who are the main characters in this story?

What are the key words and phrases in this passage?

Where does the action take place?

PART OF THE FUN OF a Sherlock Holmes mystery is the contrast between Holmes, who notices everything, and Watson, who overlooks the crucial clues or doesn't know what to do with them when he has them.

Later mystery writers have followed this same pattern to good effect. We are fascinated by observant detectives because we see how valuable their skill is and we know we don't have it.

A study group, whether it is studying the Bible or another book, needs this skill. Without accurately observing the details of what the writer has said, people often misinterpret and then misapply the text.

Unfortunately, observation is boring for many people. Observation questions can feel condescending, as though they are belaboring the obvious. There are ways, however, to ask the most important observation questions without boring or insulting the group.

START WITH YOUR OWN RESEARCH

It's not feasible to ask all potential observation questions during a group meeting. Hence, you'll need to do your own careful observation ahead of time and then select a few key questions that you think will draw out the most important things the group needs to observe in the text. Beyond those, you may find it most economical to state some of your observations on the way to asking an interpretation question (see pages 9–10). The rest of your homework will simply be for your own background information.

Journalists learn the five W's and one H that form the basis of all good reporting: Who? What? When? Where? Why? and How? As you read and reread the text, ask yourself,

- Who are the characters in the story?
- Who is the writer of the book?
- Who are the recipients of the letter?

Make a list of all the people mentioned. If necessary, look up their names in a Bible dictionary so you know who they are and whatever else the Bible says about them. Does the passage say anything descriptive about the people ("The scribes and Pharisees were *angry* . . .")?

- What are the most important words and phrases in the passage?
- What are the main events?

- What action verbs are used?
- What happens to whom?

Make another list of the key words and phrases. Notice the main nouns. Notice the verbs. Notice words that are repeated—writers often repeat words that are central to the point they want to make. Synonyms (*sin, transgression, disobedience*) are a form of repetition. Notice words that show comparison (*like, similarly*) or contrast (*however, but, much more*). Notice words that seem to carry a lot of weight in the writer's vocabulary (*kingdom, salvation, righteousness*).

- When does each event take place?
- Does the author talk about something that has happened, something that is happening, or something that will happen?

List all the references to time. Then look at your verbs and notice whether they talk about the past, the present, the future, something that started in the past but is still going on, and so on. Are any of the verbs commands? If so, what does the speaker or writer say the hearer or reader should do? When should they do it: Immediately? Constantly? Whenever they feel like it?

- Where do the events take place?
- Does it all happen in one place, or is there movement from one location to another?

List all the locations. A Bible dictionary may give you some information about them, and a Bible atlas will show you how long it would have taken to get from one place to another and what the journey might have been like. Also, does the text say anything descriptive about the places ("How *lovely* is your dwelling place . . .")?

- Why, according to the writer, did one of the characters do what she did?
- Why, according to the writer, is the reader's situation occurring?

When the writer says why something happened, that's something you observe. When you have to draw your own conclusions about why something happened, that's an interpretation. Interpretive "why" questions are fair game, but postpone them for the moment. See if the writer tells you why. ("The scribes and Pharisees were angry *because* . . .")

- How did something happen?
- How is something possible?
- How does something work?

Again, before your group tries to figure out how, see if the writer tells you how.

SELECT WHAT'S INTERESTING AND RELEVANT

Having done your sleuthing, select the information you think your group really needs to know in order to draw accurate conclusions about the text. Maybe, for the purposes of your group, it isn't that important to know where Galatia was. It's tempting to tell them anyway, since you went to the trouble of finding out, but resist that temptation. Tell a friend all the great stuff you learned, and then be courteous of your group's time.

In the same way, maybe only two of the verbs in the passage are critical to the line of discussion through which you want to lead the group. The other verbs are important to the passage, but they're part of a different conversation.

Next, divide these crucial observations into two categories.

Category 1 contains the information that will be helpful for the group to draw out of the text itself.
Category 2 comprises information you will simply give the group.

For instance, when the group meets and someone has read the passage aloud, it might be most efficient for you to say,

Notice that this story is taking place in Caesarea Philippi. That's in the far north of Palestine, a long way from anywhere. Jesus has taken His disciples away on retreat.

Offering such background straightforwardly can be much more helpful than asking, "Where does this story take place?" and then "Does anybody know where Caesarea Philippi was? Why is that significant?" If nobody knows, you will have to answer your own question, and people will feel that you are playing games with them.

(Note: The last sentence of this information—"Jesus has taken His disciples away on retreat"—goes beyond observation to interpretation. You have explained the significance of the fact you've pointed out. But you've left plenty for the group to discuss; see chapter 4.)

AWARENESS VERSUS ANALYSIS

The purpose of an observation question is to promote *awareness*. Most people miss many details when they read. A fact question helps them focus in and really see.

Imagine that you are teaching someone to play tennis. You can say, "Keep your eye on the ball." The person thinks, "Thank you for that insightful advice. I never thought of watching the ball." He believes he *is* watching the ball. You can ask, "Are you watching the ball?" He might respond internally, "Of course, you idiot," or "No, I'm distracted by your dumb questions." But if you say, "How high is the ball when it passes over the net?" you have given him something to focus on. He now has something to be aware of, a reason to engage his brain and notice something that was there all the time. A good observation question draws the group's attention to facts (like the height of the ball) that are significant and worthy of focused awareness.

In chapter 4 we'll deal with questions that promote *analysis* as opposed to awareness. Analysis and awareness are different mental modes. It's difficult to do both at once. That's why you will ask people to draw out the facts (awareness) and then shift gears to consider the meaning (analysis).

RESPECTFUL FACT QUESTIONS

Having resolved to draw people's awareness to just a few crucial observations, you can then ask some questions that feel engaging and respectful, not like tests. Some standard observation questions for stories (as in the Gospels) are

- Who are the characters in this story?
- What happens in this story? Can someone quickly list the events one by one, as if you were taking snapshots?
- What important things do people in this story say to each other?
- How do people relate or respond to each other?
- What reason does Matthew give for why Jesus did this?

Some standard observation questions for passages of teaching (as in Paul's letters) are

- What are the key words in this passage?
- What words are repeated in this passage?
- What are the action words in this passage?
- What are the key points of Paul's argument in this paragraph?
- Can someone list them briefly: first this, which leads to this, which leads to this . . . ?
- According to Paul, why was a Savior necessary?

In some cases, you can make a simple observation for the group as a bridge to asking a more sophisticated one:

Paul mentions Christ eight times in this chapter. Can someone list everything Paul says about Christ here?

As a general rule, you won't ask too many "Why?" and "How?" questions at the fact-gathering stage. They tend to encourage people to shift into analysis rather than awareness. But if there are some important "why" or "how" clues stated in the text, you could draw attention to them without saying "why" or "how":

- Why: What reasons does Paul give for the hard-heartedness of humans in our natural state?
- How: What steps toward maturity does Peter outline?

Notice that none of the questions given in this chapter will normally be answered by a single word or phrase, and never by "Yes" or "No." All feel like adult questions. None of the questions belabor the obvious. You won't use all of them for any one discussion, so people won't feel that you are making them do endless baby work. In as little as five minutes, you can draw out the key details and move on to what people really want to talk about: what it all means.

4

A MATTER OF INTERPRETATION

Interpretation Questions

What does it mean?

What's the author's point?

What's the connection with what came before?

How are these two characters different?

THE MEAT OF A DISCUSSION about a text concerns its meaning. Sometimes the meaning is obvious, but often we need to dig for it. Batting around the possible interpretations of a key sentence or the possible explanations for a character's behavior is part of the fun of discussing a text.

TYPES OF INTERPRETATION QUESTIONS

What Does It Mean?

A basic, all-purpose interpretation question takes the form of

What does [the author] mean by . . . ?

This works for words, phrases, sentences, and paragraphs. You could ask the group to list (observe) everything Paul says about resurrection in 1 Corinthians 15 and then ask,

What does Paul mean by *resurrection*? How does he explain it in this passage?

Here you're asking the group to summarize their observations into a definition of a word. You could ask the same about a phrase ("the Kingdom of God") or something longer, such as the command "As the Father has sent me, I am sending you" (John 20:21).

It's often helpful to make a what-does-it-mean question as precise as possible:

Why has the Father sent Jesus? How does that relate to why Jesus has sent the disciples?

This is just a more pointed way of saying, "What does 'As the Father . . . ' mean?" You've thought about the meaning of this sentence and have decided that "As the Father has sent me" means in part "For the same reason that the Father has sent me." Then you've asked about that reason or purpose.

Your goal here is to ask about the precise issue you want to discuss (the Father's purpose) without asking a question that puts words into anyone's mouth (see page 7).

How Is It Significant?

Most observation questions will be followed by some form of

How is that significant?

For instance, having invited the group to observe that Paul repeats the word *comfort* nine times in various forms throughout 2 Corinthians 1:3-7, you'll want to ask how that repetition is significant. What does it say about Paul's meaning in this passage? How does it reveal the main point of the paragraph?

In the same way, having identified that the key verbs in Ephesians 1:3-14 are all in some form of the past tense, you'll want to ask what that observation says about the meaning of this passage:

Q: What's the significance of all these past-tense verbs?
A: These are all things that God has already done for us, not things we're waiting for Him to do.

From there you're set up for the first stage of application: So what? (See chapter 7.)

What's the Point?

When Jesus told a story, He did it to drive home a single important point. You might ask,

What point is Jesus making in the parable of the mustard seed?

You could help the group a little by focusing that question more precisely:

What point is Jesus making about the Kingdom in the parable of the mustard seed?

Sometimes it's helpful to draw attention to the audience Jesus is addressing. Here's an observation question followed by an interpretation question:

> Q: When Jesus told the stories about the lost sheep, lost coin, and lost son in Luke 15, who was He talking to?
> A: The Pharisees and teachers of the law, who were complaining about Jesus' behavior toward sinners.
> Q: What was Jesus saying to the Pharisees and teachers in these three stories?

We can also ask, "What's the point?" about most of Jesus' one-liners and pithy sayings:

> What point was Jesus making to the woman's accusers with His comment about who should throw the first stone?

Sometimes it's possible to ask, "What's the point?" about a story told by one of the Gospel writers, or the writer of Genesis, or another narrative book. But we have to be cautious because the writer may not be trying to make one simple point in a given story. He may be saying something about God, and something about the shaping of Israel, and something about evil in the world. Still, you can always ask,

> What point does this story make about God?

This question doesn't rule out other truths one could draw from the text; it simply focuses on one of them.

You can also ask, "What's the point?" about a prophecy of Isaiah or a line of reasoning in Romans. Having observed the key phrases and discussed their meaning, you can ask what Paul's overall point in the chapter is. In this case, "What's the point?" is a way of summarizing the meaning of a passage. (For more on summarizing, see chapter 6.)

How Are They Alike? How Are They Different?

Like repetition and key words, comparison and contrast are important clues to the meaning of a story or argument. You can invite the group to find these in a wide-open way:

- What comparisons does Paul make in this passage?
- What contrasts do you observe in this story?

Or you can focus your question more precisely to give the group some help:

- What are all the differences between flesh and spirit that Paul mentions here?
- How is Mary's response to the angel different from Zechariah's?
- What is similar about the way Jesus deals with each of these people?

What's the Cause? What's the Result?

Alternatively, the meaning of a passage may have to do with cause and effect. For instance, 2 Samuel 11–20 recounts a series of events, each of which sets others in motion, sometimes years later. King David decides he's getting too old to go soldiering with his men. He's hanging around the palace and decides to commandeer Bathsheba, the wife of one of his officers. That fateful decision leads to her pregnancy. Learning of her pregnancy, David decides to engineer her husband's death so he can marry her. This decision produces a murder, a marriage, and the death of David and Bathsheba's child.

Not long after, David's eldest son, Amnon, decides to rape his half sister, Tamar. The text invites us to ask,

> To what degree do you think David's example of sexual immorality influenced his son's behavior?

Incredibly, David decides not to punish Amnon's crime, to pretend this terrible deed against his daughter never happened. So we ask,

- Why do you suppose David doesn't punish Amnon? (cause)
- What are the results of this decision? (effect)

Next, Tamar's brother Absalom decides to take matters into his own hands; he murders Amnon. David handles this murder poorly, unwilling either to punish or to face Absalom.

- Why do you think David has so much trouble dealing with his son the murderer? (cause)
- What are the results of David's failure this time? (effect)

Absalom continues to bear a grudge against his father, and the eventual result is that Absalom conspires to usurp his father's throne, rapes his father's concubines, tears the nation apart in civil war, and finally dies a violent death. David has lost three sons, a daughter, and a great deal of self-respect. Tracing this chain of rapes, murders, and their consequences offers keen insight into family dynamics and the effects of moral choices.

Teaching passages can also revolve around cause and effect. When a sentence is structured around "If . . . then," the "if" clause tells the cause (or condition) and the "then" clause tells the effect. Sometimes "then" is implied but not stated: "If we walk in the light, as he is in the light, [then] we have fellowship with one another, and the blood of Jesus, his Son, purifies us from all sin" (1 John 1:7). You might ask,

What cause and effect does this statement set up?

Or more precisely,

What are the results of walking in the light?

Or

What makes genuine fellowship possible, according to John?

Other linking words, such as *therefore*, *since*, and *because*, are also clues to cause and effect: "Therefore, since we have been justified through faith, we have peace with God. . . . And we boast . . ." (Romans 5:1-2). You can ask,

What results of justification does Paul name?

What's the Connection?

Some passages stand on their own, unconnected to what precedes or follows them. This is generally true in Proverbs. In most writing, however, biblical or otherwise, ideas are connected. The letters of Paul are composed of paragraphs—units of thought that build from idea to idea to idea. Paul makes a point. Then he says, "Therefore God . . ." A few sentences later he writes, "Because of this, God . . ." So it's appropriate to ask,

- What's the connection between this paragraph and what Paul says in the previous one?
- What's the connection between this paragraph and what follows?

You're asking the group to trace Paul's argument.

Likewise, events in a story are usually connected, often by cause and effect, sometimes by comparison or contrast.

- What connection might there be between the seduction and murder described in 2 Samuel 11 and the rapes and murder described in 2 Samuel 13 and 16?
- Chapter 11 represents a turning point in the story of David. How is what follows different from what came before?
- How is the woman's response to Jesus different from Jairus's response?
- What's the connection among the three parables Jesus tells in Matthew 21:28 through 22:14? What's the connection between those three parables and the events going on around Jesus at this point in the story?

In Old Testament narrative, the units of thought are events. In the Gospels, the units are the little scenes or individual teachings. In the letters, the units of thought are paragraphs. In the Prophets, the units are called oracles. Isaiah 5:1-7 is one oracle, one whole speech that Isaiah presumably delivered at one time. We can ask,

> How does Isaiah 5:1-7 fit into the overall theme of
> these early chapters of Isaiah?

As poetry, the Psalms are often made up of verses or stanzas. We can ask how one stanza (group of verses) is connected to or contrasts with the one that precedes or follows it.

How Would You Describe Him or Her?

If you're studying a story, it's always interesting to ask people to describe the characters.

- What kind of a guy is Peter?
- What qualities do you observe in Ruth?
- What do you like about Zacchaeus? What don't you like?
- What aspects of God's personality does this story reveal?
- What are Abraham's motives in this situation?
- What does John value? What's important to him?
- What is Jacob primarily battling against throughout this tale?

These are the same kinds of questions you'd use to discuss a novel or a film: the motives, values, strengths, weaknesses, and central conflicts of the characters.

WHAT DO YOU THINK?

Observation is about facts. Interpretation is often about opinions. The writer of 2 Samuel doesn't state as fact that David's adultery and murder affected his sons' behavior and his own responses to their behavior. We get a strong hint in 2 Samuel 12:10-12, when the prophet Nathan tells David that because of his crimes, the sword will never depart from his house, calamity will come upon him out of his own household, and he will suffer the same shame of sexual theft he inflicted upon Bathsheba's husband. Ultimately, however, we are putting two and two together and drawing our own conclusions.

Asking for group members' opinions is a fine thing. In order to distinguish between facts and opinions, it's often helpful to designate opinion questions in one of these ways:

- Why do you think . . . ?
- What do you think . . . means?
- Why do you suppose . . . ?
- What might you conclude from . . . ?

This kind of phrasing makes it clear that you're asking about an area in which reasonable people might disagree, and it's appropriate for group members to have differing views. If you ask people to explain their views, you can get a lively conversation going.

Of course, opinion isn't the same as wild speculation. You're asking people to draw educated conclusions based on the available data. But even questions that require a good deal of imagination can be extremely helpful:

What do you think it would have been like to be the man filled with a legion of demons, living among the tombs and cutting himself with stones?

A question like this helps people put themselves into the scene, picturing it, feeling it, even smelling it.

WARNING: ALL INTERPRETATIONS ARE NOT EQUAL

Even though opinion is fair game in interpretation, all opinions are not necessarily equal. All interpretations are not equal. That is, it's possible to be wrong about what a passage means. It's possible to read one's own prejudices into a text and miss what the writer is saying. More than a century ago, Lewis Carroll parodied the all-too-human tendency to twist words to our liking in this conversation between Alice and Humpty Dumpty in *Through the Looking-Glass*:

> "I don't know what you mean by 'glory,'" Alice said.
>
> Humpty Dumpty smiled contemptuously. "Of course you don't—till I tell you. I meant 'there's a nice knock-down argument for you!'"
>
> "But 'glory' doesn't mean 'a nice knock-down argument,'" Alice objected.
>
> "When *I* use a word," Humpty Dumpty said, in rather a scornful tone, "it means just what I choose it to mean—neither more nor less."
>
> "The question is," said Alice, "whether you *can* make words mean so many different things."
>
> "The question is," said Humpty Dumpty, "which is to be master—that's all."[1]

Humpty Dumpty didn't feel bound by the dictionary definition of the word *glory* or the rules of logic. Many people in discussion groups today feel similarly free to make up their own version of what Jesus said, or to say that "walking in the light" in 1 John 1 means whatever they want it to mean. "That's true for you, but this is true for me" is a deeply held belief for some people. The right to one's own interpretation is treated almost as a civil right, a basic human freedom.

When the text is not allowed to speak for itself, freedom is diminished, not enhanced. Why? Because interpreters with the most power inevitably win. Humpty Dumpty understood that the person with power (the "master") often claims the right to declare what words mean. Humpty thought that was just fine. But like Alice, Martin Luther complained in the sixteenth century that the people with power in the church hierarchy had read their own interpretations into biblical texts and distorted the gospel. In the nineteenth century, people with power used the Bible to justify slavery. Everyone reads a text through the lens of his or her own culture and experience, but when the rules of logic, the common meaning of words, and the original context of the writing are all thrown out the window, people usually hear only what they want to hear. That's a path you don't want your group wandering down.

Hence, when studying 1 Corinthians 15, it will be important to ask, "What does Paul mean by *resurrection*?" He makes it clear that he means something different from the immortality of the soul that many Greeks believed in, and one would have to do violence to the text in order to read reincarnation into it. People with Humpty Dumpty's interpretive skills may think they can make *resurrection* mean whatever they want, but while they can disagree with Paul, they shouldn't be allowed to distort what he is saying. (For a follow-up question that deals with opinions that distort, see page 64.)

In the case of a biblical text, it's important to consider what the passage meant in its original context—what the writer might have meant to say to the original audience—before we jump into applying it to our modern situation. (On bridging between the original purpose and the present application of a passage, see pages 74–78.)

Understanding the original meaning is not effortless. For one thing, few study groups are experts in the social customs and political intrigues of the ancient world. Hence, when we read in Luke 7:36-50 that a woman unbinds her hair, we may not automatically recognize this (as Luke's first readers would have done) as shocking behavior. For another thing, many books of the Bible are excerpts of ongoing conversations. Reading the letters of Paul, for example, is not unlike overhearing one-half of a telephone conversation. Paul said a great deal in person to the believers in Thessalonica. Then he received word of them from a messenger and wrote 1 Thessalonians in response to whatever the messenger said. We have the letter, but not the in-person discussions or the messenger's report. Then Paul received a response to his letter. In 2 Thessalonians he wrote about "the man of lawlessness" (2:3). The Thessalonians could interpret his words in light of everything else he told them. We have to interpret them in light of the rest of what we read in Scripture. Just because we have the Holy Spirit's help doesn't mean we should take the task lightly.

If your group lacks a thorough background in the whole teaching of Scripture (as most groups do), you may want to provide some of that background to the degree that it will help the group understand the text at hand. Likewise, if some information on the political tensions between Egypt and Assyria or the social significance of a woman with unbound hair would help, you might offer it at a relevant moment.

Some study guides include reference notes with just this kind of information. If you are designing your own study, you may find everything you need in a good study Bible or commentary. All study Bibles and commentaries are not equally helpful, however, so you might want to gather several recommendations before selecting one. (For more on the importance of the original context, see pages 74–78.)

Generally, a little of this kind of background information will go a long way toward helping your group make sense of a passage. From there, some good questions can guide them in their own discovery.

If the role of opinion in Bible study is much misunderstood, the role of feelings is almost never discussed. Feelings are factors in interpretation that occur whether we approve of them or not, so it makes sense to tap into the benefits they can offer while navigating around the pitfalls they can present. Chapter 5 will explore how to do that.

5

TELL US HOW YOU REALLY FEEL

Feeling Questions

How would you have felt if you had been this woman?

What do you feel when you hear Jesus say this?

I'VE NEVER SEEN A BOOK ON Bible study that addresses the role of feelings. I get the sense that some people out there can read a text, figure out what it means, and then go and do what it says without ever having to wrestle with mixed emotions about this drastic change in outlook or habit. Or they read a story in the Bible, analyze it, and draw out a lesson about God or life, but never have an emotional response to the events.

This may be a matter of personality, but it seems to me that significant numbers of us are heavily influenced by our emotional responses, whether we like it or not. We read, "You cannot serve both God and money" (Matthew 6:24). We look around at the others in our Bible study, and we smile. "Sure,

I agree with that," we say. But somewhere inside we're feeling threatened. "Easy for you to say," our stomachs are muttering, "but you don't live in modern society, where everybody I know has nice things, and where people expect me to look good at work, and where my kids need braces and would die if they didn't have the right shoes on the first day at school." If we leave that hostile emotion unexamined, it simply controls us, and we wonder why we can't manage to seek first the Kingdom of God and His righteousness (Matthew 6:33). But when we pay attention to such feelings, name them, even tell a group about them, we find ourselves more able to step back and say, "So this is what I'm feeling. Now what am I going to do? How am I going to manage this hostility, and the fears that lie behind it, so that I can do what Jesus says?"

Likewise, many of us find that the stories of the Bible sink deeper into our hearts when we let ourselves empathize with the characters, when we try to put ourselves into their shoes and imagine what they might have been feeling. When we feel the leper's loneliness and despair, then his wonderment at Jesus' compassionate touch, the story affects us more profoundly than if we simply analyze it. And when we try on Jesus' feeling of compassion, asking, "When was the last time I felt this for someone?" we begin to add an especially godlike emotion to our all-too-human repertoire of responses to people.

Asking members of a study group what they feel can sound like amateur psychotherapy, but it doesn't have to. In this chapter we'll explore appropriate ways to discuss feelings in a Bible study, as well as the role of feeling questions in caring, support, and task groups.

AIRTIME FOR EMOTIONS

Some passages are straightforward about emotions: "Therefore I tell you, do not worry about your life . . ." (Matthew 6:25). Questions for this passage might include

- What does worry feel like, in your experience?
- What are some things you are inclined to worry about?
- On a scale of 0 to 10, 0 being utterly unflappable and 10 being prone to panic attacks, how big a problem would you say worry is for you?
- What reasons for not worrying does Jesus give in this passage?
- From a logical point of view, how convincing are Jesus' reasons to you?
- From an emotional point of view, to what degree do Jesus' words help you stop worrying?
- If you were going to play devil's advocate, how would you defend your anxieties against Jesus' reasons?
- How would your life be different if you really believed Jesus' reasons in your gut?

Two of these questions invite the group to separate their logical responses (we all know at some level that Jesus is right) from their emotional responses (which might feel very different). In this way, we give people permission to listen to what their negative emotions are saying. Then, the question about defending one's anxieties invites them to listen even more closely. The flesh is no longer left to whisper covertly against the Spirit; we hand it the microphone and invite it to have its say. Now we know what we're dealing with and are better equipped to make some decisions about which voice to obey.

THE TRUTH WILL SET YOU FREE

Honesty is the best policy. When Jesus asks, "Which of you, if his son asks for bread, will give him a stone?" (Matthew 7:9), He hopes to hear, "Of course no father would do that." But the truth is, some of us in the audience are thinking something else, such as *I was seldom able to ask my father for anything, because he was never home,* or *I asked God for a husband—or a job that doesn't degrade me, or the life of my child—and God gave me a stone instead. Frankly, I'm still hurt and angry about that. That's what I feel when I read this passage.*

Jesus can deal with an honest answer like this. He will not fall off His throne. He got exasperated with the Laodiceans because they were "neither cold nor hot"—"Love me or hate me, show me some passion," He virtually shouts (Revelation 3:14-16). Giving a group member permission to say, "I'm hurt and I'm angry" may be the first step toward helping that person move past those feelings and be reconciled to God. As long as people have strong feelings like these between them and God, they are in no position to go out and apply a Bible teaching. Just as in a relationship with a human, they will find it easier to hear God once they know God has heard them.

So for Matthew 7:7-12 we might ask,

- What emotions does this passage evoke in you?
- What objections might a person raise to Jesus' picture of the good Father?

Many group members will probably express positive emotions about Jesus' words. That's helpful too. Jesus is using humorous imagery to make a point, to get people to change both their beliefs and their feelings about the Father.

EMPATHY

Empathy is the capacity to put oneself in someone else's shoes, to identify with that person's feelings or experience. It's a useful interpersonal skill, but it's also essential to a full understanding of almost any writing, biblical or otherwise. It takes no empathy to comprehend a calculus textbook, but to understand Sarah's barrenness, Jeremiah's laments, the psalmists' joy, various people's reactions to Jesus, or Paul's attitude toward the Philippians, empathy is invaluable.

There are at least two ways to ask an empathic question:

- How do you think Sarah felt when Hagar got pregnant?
- How would you have felt if you were Sarah?

In the case of Sarah, it's fairly clear from her subsequent behavior that she felt something along the lines of cheated and angry. Hence, if you asked the question in the first way above, you wouldn't be inviting wild speculation, and you probably wouldn't get a wide range of answers. Likewise, if you ask,

What do you think Paul feels toward the Philippians?

you're asking the group to add up all of Paul's expressions of joy about their friendship, his gratitude for the money they've sent, his pleasure at the maturity they're showing, and his concern for their continued growth. In other words, the group has much data to go on, and you're asking them to interpret it.

However, if a wide range of opinion is possible or likely, the formula "How would you have felt" may be preferable:

> How would you have felt if you were Mary Magdalene and had just realized that the man talking to you was Jesus, risen from the dead?

John doesn't say how Mary felt, so you might get a variety of responses: stunned, scared, incredulous, overwhelmed, thrilled, euphoric, or a combination of several feelings.

You can help people identify with the characters by painting the scene and asking your question in the present tense:

> Imagine you're the woman who has been bleeding for twelve years. You've snuck up on Jesus and touched Him, and you've felt a sudden change in your body. Now He's looking around and asking who touched Him. It's unlawful for you to have touched a rabbi like this because your bleeding has made you unclean. What are you feeling?

POSITIVE EMOTIONS

Feeling questions are not just for drawing out people's pain. When you think the writer is trying to kindle courage, humor, joy, or excitement, give group members a chance to voice those feelings.

For instance, in Romans 8:2839, Paul rises to a rhetorical crescendo in order to convince his readers that following

Christ is a glorious calling. We can imagine him pacing the room in which he is dictating, raising his voice, gesturing, his eyes glittering, while his secretary madly scribbles. He means these words to straighten our spines. Simply to analyze them is to miss the point, so we ask a question like one of these:

- What emotions do you think Paul meant these words to spark in his readers?
- What do you feel after reading/hearing that?
- How do you respond emotionally to what Paul says here?

If group members feel nothing in response to this passage, then it's at least possible that something is sapping their spiritual lives of passion.

WHAT'S A FEELING, ANYWAY?

Of course, some people aren't aware of feeling anything most of the time. Numbness is not uncommon. Some don't notice feelings other than anger or sexual arousal. Hurt, fear, and gladness embarrass some people, so they don't allow themselves to feel those emotions. Finally, some people feel many things but lack a vocabulary for naming what they feel. Any of these people may meet your feeling questions with silence. To help them out, you may want to offer some possibilities:

When I think about Jesus saying that to me, I feel . . .
- glad (excited, joyful, thrilled, hopeful, encouraged, eager)
- calm (relieved, relaxed, peaceful, content)

- afraid (anxious, nervous, worried, terrified, threatened)
- angry (mad, threatened, hostile, furious, annoyed)
- sad (depressed, discouraged, hopeless, indifferent, hurt, grief-stricken, longing)
- nothing

English offers a whole palette of feeling words with every shade of meaning; you can select three or four simple options for any given question. If you always include the option "nothing," people won't feel pressured to come up with an emotion.

FEELINGS VERSUS OPINIONS

People often confuse feelings and opinions. They may say, "I feel that Paul is right and this is what we should do." However, the phrase "I feel that . . ." introduces an opinion, not a feeling. It is equivalent to "I think that . . ." Feelings usually come out as adjectives (*happy, sad, angry, afraid*) or word pictures ("I feel as if I've just been hit by a truck").

If you're leading a support group, it would be appropriate to explain the difference between feelings and opinions. In a study group, you may want to avoid the impression that you're playing therapist. You can just rephrase the question:

I'm asking about emotional reactions. Does anyone find himself feeling mad or encouraged or nervous in response to this passage?

Eventually, people will catch on that when you say, "What do you think?" you're asking for an opinion, and when you say, "What do you feel?" you're asking for a feeling.

CARING AND SUPPORT GROUPS

Feelings play a much larger role in caring and support groups than in study or task groups. Caring and support groups both belong to a larger category that we might call relationship-focused groups—that is, the relationships among the group members are the top priority, ahead of material to study or a task to be accomplished. "Process" takes precedence over content.

By "caring group," I mean a group with a moderate level of vulnerability whose primary purpose is to provide a place where members may talk about what is happening in their personal and spiritual lives; empathize with, encourage, and pray for each other; and possibly meet some of each other's practical needs. The needs people bring to a caring group usually vary widely. By "support group," I mean a group in which the members are more frank about their personal struggles; in which they receive similar empathy, encouragement, and possibly prayer; and in which they may all be focusing on a similar set of issues. One could have a support group for recently divorced or bereaved people, for parents of teenagers, for alcoholics, or for survivors of childhood abuse, for example.

The most popular support groups of today, those based on the Twelve Steps of Alcoholics Anonymous, are not guided by leaders, and questions are against the rules. No one asks another in an AA meeting, "How did you feel when that happened?" or "What are you feeling right now?" However, in caring and support groups where there is a designated leader, such questions are usually considered appropriate.

The first arena of questioning deals with the past. A

person wants to talk about an event that happened yesterday or twenty years ago (a caring group would be more likely to stick to events of the recent past). The leader helps the person go beyond merely reporting the facts and into identifying and verbalizing his or her feelings about the event. Appropriate questions might be

- What were you feeling when that happened?
- What did you feel after it was over?
- How did that affect the way you felt/feel about yourself?
- How did that affect the way you felt/feel about the other person?
- How has that affected the way you felt/feel about God?
- What does it feel like now to have shared that?

This last question moves into the present, what is going on in the room right now. In both caring and support groups, it's helpful to check in with people on what they're feeling. This tells a leader what people might need from the group, and it encourages other group members to express empathy toward each other. Some present-oriented questions are

- What does it feel like to have shared that?
- What do you feel now about that situation as you look back on it?
- What do you feel when you think about going back into that situation?
- How do you feel about God now?
- (To the group) What feelings does Mary's story raise for others of you?

There is much more to leading a caring or support group than simply asking feeling questions, but a repertoire of such questions is among the tools that will serve such a leader well.

FEELINGS AND TASKS

Some groups, such as committees, are task groups. That is, their primary purpose is to get something done. Relationships are important but secondary to the task. Process should serve the mission, rather than being an end in itself.

Other groups, both relationship-focused and content-focused, also have tasks to accomplish. There is usually some business to be done even in a support or study group.

Feeling questions play a small but vital role in accomplishing tasks, whether in a committee or a study group. In chapter 8 and the epilogue, we will discuss how to use questions for decision-making, consensus building, and evaluation. At this point it's enough to say that when the group is doing tasks like these, checking in with people's feelings is often helpful. For instance,

- We've agreed that option A makes the most sense for us financially. How does everyone feel about option A?
- How would it feel to do X? How would it feel to do Y?
- We've spent thirty minutes talking about this. How is everyone feeling at this point? Satisfied? As if there's still some unfinished business here?
- How do you feel about the way our meeting has gone tonight?

Feelings matter, whether they're on the table or under it. People may assent to a decision based on logic, but if their unexamined feelings are telling them something else, the decision may unravel later. And feelings are an excellent cue to potential problems in the way meetings are run or relationships among group members are handled. In short, discussing feelings is an important step in the work of any group, whether you're planning an event, recovering from a loss, or applying the Scripture to your lives.

6

KEEPING THE BALL IN PLAY

Follow-Up Questions

Can you tell us more about that? Because . . . ?

Does anyone else feel the same way?

SO FAR, WE'VE DEALT WITH what are often called primary or launching questions. These put the ball in play, asking for facts, opinions, feelings, or plans of action. However, once the discussion ball is in the air, secondary or guiding questions keep it moving. They build on the primary question so the discussion resembles a good tennis match (serve, return, volley, volley, volley) instead of a dull one (serve, point; serve, point; serve, point).

Secondary questions serve many other purposes besides keeping the discussion interesting:

- They keep the group from talking just on the surface of an issue.
- They keep the group on track and moving forward.
- They help the group shift from a focus on the leader to a shared discussion.

There are many different types of secondary questions. The following work especially well.

REPHRASE THE QUESTION

It's fine to ask a thought-provoking question and be met with silence while people think through what they want to say. However, sometimes you'll ask a question and receive silence because people don't know what to say. In that case, you might rephrase or elaborate on your own question:

Q: What does it mean to be "conformed to the likeness of his Son"?
[Silence.]
Q: For instance, what qualities might that involve? Do you think we'll all be exactly alike when we're like Jesus?

You can also rephrase someone else's question or statement. Perhaps she has thought out loud for a minute or two, trying to express what she wants to say. If someone has said more than five or six sentences, it can be helpful to pull together what you think you heard:

So you're saying you don't think our sharing and prayer time is being used effectively, is that right?

PROBE FOR MORE INFORMATION

Often when people give short answers, we sense that more lies behind them. In that case, we want to probe for further information. For instance,

> Q: What picture comes to mind when you think of the word *holy*?
> A: Somebody super perfect, untouchable.
> Q: Do you think of that as a positive quality, negative, or just neutral?
> A: Well, it could be positive, but I guess it has a bit of a negative edge in my mind.
> Q: Can you say more about that?

To simply accept the first answer above without following it up with more questions might be appropriate in a warm-up question, but when you're really discussing a subject like holiness, you want to get beneath the surface of an answer like that. You want to know why the person has responded as he has.

Please notice that neither of the follow-up questions was "Why?" Why not? Because "Why?" and "Why not?" tend to put people on the defensive. They feel you're asking them to defend their answer, that perhaps they've said something wrong or stupid. "Why on earth do you think that?!" When someone risks hinting that *holy* feels a bit negative (when we all know it's supposed to be a good word), he wants to know it was safe to do so. Therefore, the two secondary questions both get at "Why?" in gentler ways. The first is quite specific, giving the person three possible answers. The second is completely open-ended.

You'll often see "Why or why not?" in a printed study guide. This formula isn't too bad in print, but in person it works much better to say something like

- Because . . . ?
- Can you tell us more about that?
- That's interesting. What leads you to that conclusion?
- That's great. Can you talk about how you came to realize that?
- Interesting. What does the text say about that?

This last formula, "What does the text say about that?" is helpful when you think someone has put forth an opinion that distorts the text (see pages 45–47). When someone gives an off-the-wall opinion, the best follow-up is often simply to ask what others think. There's usually no need to contradict the person directly—poor ideas usually die on their own. But if the whole group seems to be going off in a nonsensical direction, "What does the passage say about that?" can bring them back to the text.

Besides using variations on "Why?" you can also probe deeper with questions based on "How?" such as

- How has that affected your relationship with God/ your husband/your kids?
- How did you deal with that at the time?

(See "asking for opinions," page 44, and "asking about feelings," pages 55–58.)

PERSONALIZE

Sometimes you can get a discussion going at a safe level by talking about what people in general think or do. Then you can take it a notch deeper by asking the group what they, personally, think or do in this area. Jesus used this technique with His disciples:

"Who do people say the Son of Man is?"
They replied, "Some say John the Baptist; others say Elijah; and still others, Jeremiah or one of the prophets."
"But what about you?" he asked. "Who do you say I am?"
MATTHEW 16:13-15

ASK FOR CLARIFICATION

If someone's answer was especially long, if you don't understand it, or if you think some in the group might not understand it, you can ask for clarification:

So are you saying that you think we're spending too much time discussing prayer requests and not enough time actually praying?

Here, you've put into your own words what you think the person said. Paraphrasing like this at judicious moments can avoid miscommunications. This is an especially useful tool when you want to help the group work through an issue on which they disagree. During conflict, clarity is of nearly utmost importance—second only to charity.

INVITE OTHERS' INPUT

The leader's goal in a discussion group is to help group members talk to each other. In a new group where members don't know each other, it's common for the group process to look like a series of one-on-one conversations between the leader and one member after another, something like this:

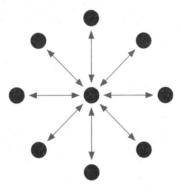

The leader asks a question, and someone answers. The leader asks another question, and someone else answers. And so on. This Q-and-A quickly becomes tiresome.

As soon as possible, an effective leader will move the group toward a process that looks more like this:

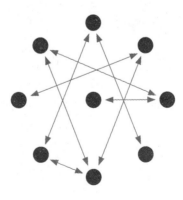

This is how a conversation over the dinner table looks: Everyone talks to everyone, and the leader falls into the background. Secondary questions that invite the rest of the group to respond to someone's statement are a key method by which the leader helps the group make this shift.

> Q: What do you think Jesus means in verse 10 by "life . . . to the full?"
> (One person answers, then the rest are silent.)
> Q: Anybody else?

"Anybody else" invites the rest of the group to add their answers to the question you just asked. Some other formulations of the same question are

- Has anyone else had a similar experience?
- What do the rest of you think?
- Does anyone have more to add?
- How have others of you dealt with significant losses?

These last two formulations also have the flavor of encouraging the group to say what they think about the first person's answer. If you want to be especially clear about asking people to comment on someone else's response, you can say,

- Kendall, what do you think about what Gerry just said?
- Does anyone have another point of view on this?
- Jan, has your experience been like Gerry's or different?

SUMMARIZE

Asking people to summarize fosters clarity. You can ask a person to summarize the last five, ten, or even thirty minutes of discussion:

- How would you summarize Paul's argument in this chapter in a sentence?
- Can someone summarize the conclusions we've drawn so far?
- Returning to our original question, "What does it mean to be called by God?" what can we conclude?

In addition, you can ask someone to paraphrase what she heard another group member saying:

Chris has raised some serious issues. Who would like to restate for us briefly what you heard her say?

At times you may want to summarize a discussion yourself with a statement rather than a question:

So the main thing Jesus is after in this passage is . . .

TEST FOR CONSENSUS OR DECISION

When discussing an issue that requires a decision, the time will come when the group must decide. At this point, it's appropriate to break in with a question like

Are we saying that prayer requests will be limited to one sentence, and additional information will either be said in prayer or discussed when we break for coffee? Is that okay with everyone?

(For more on decision-making, see pages 88–90.)

THE KEY: LISTENING

You can plan a list of primary questions ahead of your group meeting, but secondary questions have to come to you in the moment, in response to whatever the group does. Doing this effectively doesn't ultimately depend on your memorizing all the possible kinds of questions. If you relax and really listen to what people are saying, secondary questions will begin occurring to you naturally.

In fact, there may be no more valuable skill for a discussion leader than listening. When we're nervous about our performance as leaders, it's easy to focus all of our attention on the questions we are going to ask. I get the sense that Jesus was never worried about His performance, never concerned that He have a follow-up question on the tip of His tongue, so He was able to listen closely to the answer someone gave to His question. Listening requires concentration, practice, and a lack of anxiety. It helps if we are comfortable with a pause between someone's answer and our follow-up question because then we'll have time to listen carefully and then reflect on what follow-up would be most helpful to the group. Are we most concerned with how we look or with what the group needs? Effective listening and questioning requires the latter attitude.

7

SO WHAT?

Application Questions

*What do you think Jesus wanted His audience
to do in response to this parable?*

In what ways is our situation like that of the disciples in this passage?

How have you changed as a result of studying Ephesians?

What do you want to do about that?

How are Jesus' words relevant to what we do together as a group?

ONE OF THE MOST OFT-QUOTED passages in the Bible study business is James 1:22-25 (NRSV):

> But be doers of the word, and not merely hearers
> who deceive themselves. For if any are hearers of the
> word and not doers, they are like those who look at
> themselves in a mirror; for they look at themselves
> and, on going away, immediately forget what they
> were like. But those who look into the perfect law, the
> law of liberty, and persevere, being not hearers who
> forget but doers who act—they will be blessed in their
> doing.

To study the Bible or to take a class on prayer or discuss compassion for the poor—but not do anything about what one has learned—is a waste.

The Word of God holds up a mirror in which we can see our own faces: our character, values, attitudes, and habits. It offers us a perspective on our situations and relationships that we can't get on our own. At the same time, it opens up a window into the realm of God, a window in which we see the face of Christ looking back at us. We get to compare our faces to that of Christ, noting the similarities and differences. One of the many audacious claims of the gospel is that it is actually possible, by gazing consistently into that mirror and acting on what we observe by the power of the Holy Spirit, to allow God to change our faces. It is actually possible to be more like Christ at a heart level a year from now than we are today.

This is no small offer. Some recent psychological research suggests that people's personalities and character are wet cement before age eight, and up to about age twenty-five the cement is still fairly pliable. However, these studies find that most people don't change much after age twenty-five, even if they go through significant trauma. Some people are shattered by life events, but only a few grow and transform dramatically during the decades of adulthood. Even extensive psychotherapy doesn't change most people all that much. In other words, personal growth doesn't just happen. Consistent growth is truly rare. When it does happen, something on the order of a miracle is occurring. But the gospel insists that the Spirit of God—through the Word of God and with the help of the people of God—can and will perform this miracle in any person willing to cooperate.

It's worth emphasizing this fact because so many study groups settle for educating people *about* God and the Christian life. Many people don't believe it's possible for them—ordinary, full of faults—to become like Jesus. Many others like the idea in theory, but the actual process of it scares them. Do we really want to take a hard look at ourselves in the mirror, week after week? Can we bear to contemplate the face of Christ? Do we really want to give up our well-worn paths and strike out on the uncharted seas of God's ways? Do we really want the Spirit breaking up our cemented habits with a jackhammer?

If your group is made up of people absolutely committed to becoming like Christ and helping each other do so, you are blessed. More likely, though, your group contains decent people who sort of want to follow Christ but aren't eager to see their lives disrupted. They are busy people who have jobs and families, bills and housework, that don't leave them hours and hours to contemplate the face of Christ and their own hearts. Discussion questions that invite them to apply the Word of God to their lives, then, need to take into account both the mandate of the gospel (big changes) and the realities of the human condition (big obstacles to change).

SLOW AND DEEP

Instinct tells me that people who are asked to take drastic action too often and in too many different directions eventually go numb in order to survive. Consider the person who hears a Sunday sermon, reads the Bible even once or twice a week, and attends a weekly small-group meeting. If she encounters three, four, or more calls in one week to change herself drastically, she'll be overwhelmed.

Nobody can give serious attention to changing her parenting, addressing the plight of the poor, overcoming her tendency toward worry, and cultivating a more contemplative life all in one week. That's too much even for one month. People learn to tune out the guilt feelings triggered by such calls.

Consequently, my own tendency in a small group is to ask, "So what?" regularly and systematically, but to ask, "Now what?" sparingly, yet with focus and detail when I do ask it. "So what?" invites group members to think about the implications of what they are studying. "Now what?" asks them to take action individually or together, to do something concrete about those implications. "So what?" is theoretical, general application. "Now what?" is practical, specific application. "So what?" helps people think an issue through. "Now what?" guides them step-by-step in a realistic plan to be doers of the Word.

"So what?" questions work in at least two dimensions. The first dimension is *when*—helping the group bridge the gap between when the passage was written (then) and our current situation today (now). The second dimension is *who*—discerning how a passage applies to people in general, to them as individuals, or to them as a group.

THEN AND NOW

One common error in Bible study is to assume unreflectively that something God told someone to do in 605 BC is what God wants each of us to do today. A related error is to assume that God wants us to imitate everything the first Christians did without regard to the differences of situation. These errors overlook the fact that God deals both in timeless principles and in unique situations.

"You shall have no other gods before me" (Exodus 20:3) is a timeless principle. "Go from your country, your people and your father's household" (Genesis 12:1) is an instruction to a particular person, Abram. When we get the particular and the timeless confused, then we may conclude that God wants all men everywhere to be circumcised and all women everywhere to cover their heads. We may conclude, like many nineteenth-century Americans, that because Paul treated slavery as okay in AD 50, it was still okay in AD 1850. We may decide that since God told Joshua to practice genocide against the utterly degenerate Canaanites, then maybe our enemies deserve genocide and maybe we have been called by God to imitate Joshua. Over the centuries, Christians have made a few whopping errors in applying the Bible, and we do well to take those cases to heart.

Thus, "So what?" questions always begin with *then*. The first "So what?" question should point to the original purpose of the writer or speaker in the passage:

- What do you think Jesus wanted His audience to do in response to this parable?
- What action does Paul tell the Galatians to take?

With a story, it may be more helpful to ask about how the various characters respond to the challenge they face:

- How did Abram deal with his doubts?
- How did the apostles handle the conflict between the Greek-speaking believers and the Aramaic-speaking believers?

Next we look for bridges between *then* and *now* by asking how our situation is like and unlike the situation addressed in the passage:

- What conflicts do we face in our ministry? In what ways do they resemble the conflict described in Acts 6? In what ways are they different?
- Do you identify with the Galatians in any ways? In what ways are you similar or different?

Sometimes your group won't have time to explore the differences—after all, it's the similarities, or the "resonance" between *then* and *now*, that will lead to helpful application. But as the leader, you should always ask yourself, *How is our situation different?* This question will help you guide the group away from erroneous applications. Joshua's conquest of Canaan was in many ways a unique situation. The founding of the first Christian community in Jerusalem was also unique in many ways. Likewise, your little group, which might be a beachhead of Christ-following computer coders in a large software company, is unique in some ways and like all other Christian communities in other ways.

(By the way, notice that the question "Do you identify with the Galatians?" allows people to say no. Yes-or-no questions are usually to be avoided, but in this case, it would be a leading question to assume that everybody in the group is wishy-washy like the Galatians. The follow-up question "In what ways . . ." makes this a discussion question.)

For more on yes-or-no and leading questions, see pages 6–7.

Finally, with the similarities and differences between *then* and *now* in mind, we can ask whether the passage offers any timeless (*always*) principles:

What can we learn about good and poor ways of handling doubt from Abram's example?

Principles can include a sin to avoid, a promise to trust, an example to follow, a command to obey, or a truth to believe. It's essential, though, not to generalize a universal principle from a specific situation without careful thought about the differences between *then* and *now*.

So we've looked at three kinds of questions:

- the original purpose (*then*)
- the bridge of similarities (*then and now*)
- the timeless principle (*always*)

For instance, let's say you're studying 1 Corinthians 11:1-16. You've done your homework and given your group the cultural background on this difficult passage: In Jewish culture, only a prostitute would go out in public with her head uncovered. In Greek culture, women often worshiped with uncovered heads. This difference was causing strife in the Corinthian community. After giving this background, you've drawn out the facts from the text and discussed their meaning. You've decided that the passage is about appropriateness in worship. Then you can ask,

- What do you conclude was Paul's goal in telling the women of Corinth to cover their heads in worship meetings? (original purpose)

- In what ways is our situation in worship similar to the one Paul was addressing? In what ways is our situation different? (bridge of similarities)
- What principles for conducting worship meetings can we derive from this passage? (timeless principle)

YOU AND US

Once you have the bridge between then and now, and perhaps also a timeless principle, you're ready to ask people to get personal:

- How are these principles relevant to our worship in our group?
- How are these principles relevant to the way you conduct yourself in worship?
- How could we apply these principles in our church body?

Sometimes you'll want to help people apply the passage to their personal lives. At other times, you'll draw out a group application. Most of the Bible was written not to individuals but to groups. The *you* in many passages is plural. Hence, both individual and group applications are important because God is interested in transforming both individuals and communities.

Another way of asking "So what?" is to point people toward listening to the Holy Spirit:

- What do you sense the Holy Spirit is saying to us about how we relate to others in our lives who don't know Christ?
- What is one key truth from this passage that you sense the Spirit is urging you to embrace?

It's important not to talk about the Holy Spirit in a clichéd way—that's not far from taking the Lord's name in vain. But it's helpful to prompt the group to think of the Spirit who is speaking to them and who waits for them to listen quietly. Set aside fifteen minutes at the end of a group meeting to contemplate a question like one of these. Pray, asking the Spirit to speak. Then talk—with ears open.

NOW WHAT?

"So what?" questions are general questions. They ask for relevance. "Now what?" questions are pointed, asking for action.

- How can you put this insight into practice this week?
- What can you do to cultivate this into a habit?
- What will it mean, in practical terms, for you to seek God's Kingdom first this week?
- How can we, as a group, obey Isaiah's call to a true fast?

Many of your discussions will end with "So what?" questions. It is not a waste of time to help people think and feel more biblically. But sometimes, action is called for.

"Now what?" questions require specific, realistic, and measurable answers. *Specific* means that definite actions, rather than general goals, are specified. *Realistic* means that the person has devised a plan he can reasonably carry out within the limitations of his life, with the power of the Holy Spirit and the help of the group to back him up. *Measurable* means something concrete will be done, and at the end of a month or a year, the shift in the person's attitudes will be noticeable by an observant outsider. We shouldn't become obsessed with measuring spiritual growth, since the most important changes are internal and may take time to affect behavior dramatically, but it is possible to ask ourselves,

> What can I do to become a significantly more compassionate person by this time next year?

Here is a plan that is specific, realistic, and measurable:

> I think that for me, the number one barrier to relationship is my tendency to hold on to wrongs done against me and to keep score. I expect others to earn their way back into my good graces. I am going to memorize Matthew 6:14-15 and recite it to myself each morning. Each evening before I go to bed, I'm going to review the day and see when I have had a forgiving spirit toward others and when I have "kept a record of wrongs." Then I'll decide if I need to speak to the person about the matter or just let it go. Dave in this group is going to check with me by phone every couple of days for the next month to see how I'm doing on developing this quality of forgiveness.[1]

Notice that this plan involves prayer, self-examination, and accountability over the course of a month. It would be unreasonable to ask group members to come up with a new plan of this kind every week. But if a group sets aside one meeting every other month to ask "Now what?" about whatever the group has been studying for the past eight weeks or so, the results may be far more fruitful than treating "Now what?" as an afterthought at the end of each meeting. Time can be set aside at the beginning or end of each meeting for group members to tell how they are doing with their chosen plans. They can receive encouragement and support, or they can discuss a change in plans.

Alternatively, a group can set aside a meeting or part of a meeting to plan how to put what they are learning into practice as a group.

- How can our prayer time as a group better reflect what we have been learning about prayer?
- How can we together practice the kind of fasting Isaiah describes: loosening the chains of injustice and setting the oppressed free?
- What do you think about brainstorming a list of things we could do and then choosing one?

In chapter 2 (pages 20–22) we saw that questions about the future are often more intimate than those about the past or present. Most people don't talk about their hopes and goals casually. Consequently, when the group has been together for about six sessions or more, members will find it extremely bonding to begin discussing their hopes for who they want to become and how they plan to pursue their goals. Many people have other places in which to talk about what is wrong with their lives, but a place to share hope and "spur one another on toward love and good deeds" (Hebrews 10:24) is rare and priceless. One way of formulating this question is

In what ways do you want to be different as a result of our studying Philippians?

COUNTING THE COST

Jesus told a parable about two sons, in which one son agreed to do what his father asked but then didn't follow through while the other balked but eventually obeyed (Matthew 21:28-32). People frequently talk about how a passage applies to them but don't do anything about it after the discussion. One reason for this is that they don't consider the risks and costs of living the gospel. Jesus urged His followers to count the cost and to be sure they knew what they were getting themselves into before embracing the Kingdom of God. Here are some questions you can use when studying a passage that you know asks something difficult, such as turning the other cheek:

- What are the risks of doing what Jesus says here?
- What would it cost you to do that?
- What obstacles hinder you from living that way consistently?

Then, having looked squarely at the downside, invite people to weigh it against the upside:

- What would be the benefits of living like this?
- What would motivate a person to take those risks?
- How can you overcome those obstacles? How can we help?

A TYPICAL SESSION

Here is how the various kinds of questions we've addressed in this book so far might fit together into a group meeting:

- a storytelling question
- ask someone to read the Bible passage
- a fact question or two (key words, main characters, et cetera)
- what does it mean?
- maybe a follow-up question
- what do you think?
- a follow-up question or two
- another fact question
- compare/contrast
- one or two follow-up questions
- how do you feel about that?
- so what?
  the original purpose?
  the similarities between then and now?
  any timeless principles?
- what are the costs?
- now what?
  what will you do?
  how can we help?

Of course, the order here isn't rigid and some items may be omitted. But this is one possible outline.

Facts, meaning, response—that's the basic format for the study portion of a meeting. However, no group merely studies. Every group has decisions to make, even if they are as simple as what to study next. What do you do when you're trying to decide what course of action to take as a group? Whether you're a study group or a committee, chapter 8 offers some guidelines for effective problem-solving and decision-making.

8

DECISIONS, DECISIONS

Problem-Solving Questions

EVERY GROUP MAKES DECISIONS. It must decide on its purpose and goals, on ground rules for acceptable and unacceptable behavior, and on who is responsible for what. A task group may want to decide on how to train leaders for a small-group program. A caring group may need to decide how to respond to a member's illness. A study group may have to decide what to study next. This chapter will offer some guidance for arriving at the best possible decisions.

THE PROCESS OF PROBLEM-SOLVING

A decision is the product of a problem-solving process. Effective problem-solving includes these steps:

- defining the problem or issue
- identifying possible courses of action
- weighing the pros and cons of each course of action
- arriving at some level of agreement as to which course of action will best achieve the group's goals

Define the Problem

Groups often skip lightly over the first step: defining the problem. But this step can make or break the process. Suppose, for example, that the committee overseeing the small-group ministry has on its agenda "Leader Training." In previous years, potential leaders have been trained in a weekend workshop that included lecture interspersed with small-group sessions. One way to define the problem would be

When and how shall we run our weekend workshop this fall?

However, this definition assumes that several prior questions aren't even up for discussion, such as

- Do we need to train new leaders this fall?
- What is the best way for us to train leaders this year? Is there a better alternative than our weekend workshop format?
- Do we want to hold just one training this fall, or do we need more than one before Christmas?

As a general rule, it's a good idea for the discussion facilitator to state the problem as broadly as possible, then to guide the group in examining its assumptions and deciding on the problem it wants to address. The attitude "We've always done it that way" is destructive to a group's creativity and productivity in the long run.

Identify Possible Courses of Action

Philosopher Émile Chartier said, "Nothing is more dangerous than an idea when it is the only one you have." Nobel Prize winner Linus Pauling agreed: "The best way to get a good idea is to get a lot of ideas."[1] Out of any hundred ideas, maybe eighty are duds, twenty are worth a second look, eight are worth careful examination, and one is a gem. Unfortunately, nobody has figured out how to come up with that one without sorting through the other ninety-nine. Maybe God gets good ideas every time, but nobody else does.

Most group members are terrified of looking foolish. Who wants to propose an idea and have everyone else roll their eyes to the ceiling in unison? So it's up to the leader to create a space of time during the meeting when people can put on their idea-generating hats and brainstorm as many ideas as possible. For fifteen minutes, for instance, group members will suggest every possible way of training leaders they can think of. Everyone is wearing her idea hat; critic hats are saved for later. There will be no witty remarks or eloquent body language about someone's idea, no matter how wild it is. For fifteen minutes, nobody gets to say, "That's too expensive," "We don't have the personnel for that," or "We tried that three years ago, and it flopped." Questions for clarification or suggestions for improving upon someone else's ideas are postponed. Someone is assigned the task of listing all of the ideas on a flip chart, or else each person is writing ideas in eight words or less on sheets of paper that will be posted on the wall.

Weigh the Pros and Cons

Now ask the group to take off their idea hats and put on their critic hats. (I've actually heard of a group that uses real hats: green for ideas, red for evaluating ideas, and so on.) Examine each idea for its advantages and disadvantages. Invite facts, opinions, and feelings, but be clear on which is which. An unsubstantiated gut-level response is valuable as long as it's clearly labeled as intuition rather than analysis.

Ideally, you'll have a mix of people who are good at facts and feelings, analysis and intuition, details and the big picture, so you can come at the problem from many angles.

Decide

A *decision* implies that some agreement prevails among group members as to which of several courses of action is the most desirable for achieving the group's goals.[2]

There are many ways to arrive at a decision, and one decision each group makes is how to make decisions. Some possibilities are

- The leader does the research and makes the decision, and the group goes along.

- The group thoroughly discusses the options, and then the leader (or coleaders) makes the decision.

- The group gives the responsibility and authority to make the decision to the member or members who have the most expertise.

- Members are polled individually as to their preferences, and the most popular option wins.

- Members vote, and the majority rules.

- A few members with forceful personalities convince the others to go along.

- Someone flips a coin or draws lots.

- The group asks another group what it is doing, and does the opposite.

- Members discuss the options until everyone has had a chance to participate fully and the group has arrived at a consensus.

- The group postpones the decision until something happens by default.

Decisions by leaders or experts are efficient in the sense that they can be made quickly—this is an advantage during wartime or other emergency situations. However, leader-made decisions have at least two disadvantages: The leader or expert may not evaluate the data as well as the whole group; and the other group members may not commit themselves fully to a decision they did not help make. When leaders have the authority to make the decisions and the ultimate responsibility for success or failure (as in business or on a church staff), part of the job of good leaders is to discern when they really do know better than their subordinates and when they don't.

Majority vote is a time-honored method in democratic societies, so many groups take it for granted. However, at the national level, the voices of minorities are protected by ground rules such as the Constitution and Bill of Rights of the United States. In a committee or study group, there may be no such safeguards. Also, voting lends itself to choice between just two options; it is much more difficult to vote when three or more options are available. Finally, voting can split a group into "winners" and "losers."

Consequently, when every member's commitment to the decision is essential, then it is often worth the time to talk through the options until the group reaches consensus. Perfect consensus means that every group member is fully convinced that the right decision has been reached. Perfect consensus is rare, but in a group where communication is sufficiently open and the atmosphere is sufficiently supportive, it's possible to reach a workable consensus in which all members feel they have had enough input into the decision and are willing to give the decision a genuine try.

> To achieve consensus, members must have enough
> time to state their views and, in particular, their
> opposition to other members' views. By the time the
> decision is made they should be feeling that others
> really do understand them. Group members, therefore,
> must listen carefully and communicate effectively.
> . . . In reaching consensus, group members need to
> see differences of opinion as a way of (1) gathering
> additional information, (2) clarifying issues, and
> (3) forcing the group to seek better alternatives.[3]

OBSTACLES TO EFFECTIVE PROBLEM-SOLVING

Fear of Controversy

This problem-solving process is alien to many groups. In some study groups, for example, when it's time to decide on what the group will study next, the leader raises the issue and someone suggests an idea: "How about spiritual gifts?" Immediately, a common group norm kicks in and determines the other members' responses. That norm is

Avoid conflict.

Everyone talks about the positive aspects of this option. No one wants to propose an alternative for fear he will be perceived as unkind toward the person who suggested spiritual gifts and selfish about getting his own way. Perhaps some brave (or curmudgeonly) soul will say, "You know, I'm really tired of spiritual gifts." Other members feel discomfort. The defined problem shifts from "What shall we study next?" to "How can we escape this conflict without hurting anybody's feelings?"

The belief that conflict is bad usually causes groups to censor disagreement and make quick compromises. Since the Bible is full of warnings against quarreling and factions, many Christians assume they should avoid all controversy. But groups may benefit from understanding the differences among controversy, debate, fighting, and concurrence seeking.

Controversy occurs "when one group member's ideas, information, conclusions, theories, and opinions are incompatible with those of another, and the two seek to reach an agreement."[4] The group encourages people to contribute all available information and points of view, and everyone's goal is the highest possible quality of decision. People challenge each other's views respectfully and clearly, without challenging them as people but also without evading disagreement. Group members are genuinely curious to know what the others think and are genuinely open to the possibility that someone else may have a better idea than they do. This kind of controversy is usually extremely valuable for weighing the pros and cons of various alternatives and arriving at a high-quality consensus.

Debate happens when group members' ideas, information, and so on are incompatible; each person argues for her position; and a winner is declared on the basis of whose position is best. Either the leader or the rest of the group may declare the winner. In debate, the partisans are interested in winning, not in understanding the other's point of view or in reaching agreement. There are times when setting up a formal debate can help clarify the strengths and weaknesses of two views. Sometimes people really are convinced of their differing interpretations of a passage of Scripture, for example, and it can be helpful to let both sides air their views and receive the group's evaluation. However, debate can often work against warm interpersonal relationships among group members. At its extreme, debating becomes fighting when, in addition to arguing for their positions, the partisans attack each other personally.

Concurrence seeking exists when group members inhibit discussion to avoid disagreements. People compromise quickly and emphasize the areas in which they agree. This strategy appears to serve warm interpersonal relationships, but in fact it hinders people from feeling truly safe in the group, safe enough to say what they really think. Also, it keeps the group from generating lots of ideas and evaluating them thoroughly.

Obviously, I am a fan of controversy that aims toward consensus. It takes time. It takes courage, respect, careful thought, the willingness to listen, and the humility to accept that one might be wrong. In short, it takes maturity. But the results are worth the effort. A process that builds spiritual maturity and fosters high-quality decisions deserves a little cheerleading.

Other Obstacles

Plenty of other factors can derail effective problem-solving. First, members may have different goals. With different goals, they will define the problem differently. Sometimes a person's unacknowledged goal is to sabotage the group, to gain control of the group, or to get attention. Destructive goals can't possibly lead to constructive decisions.

Other factors have to do with the maturity of members. For instance, if group members lack the capacity to view a problem from a variety of points of view, they will be unable to evaluate various options and may view any controversy as a debate they intend to win. What can you do with people who are never wrong?

Sometimes the individual members of a group may be mature, but because the group as a whole is young, members haven't had time to build trust and understand how the others communicate. People often need time and experience together in order to become an effective problem-solving team.

Finally, airtime needs to be well distributed. The leader may need to draw out shy members actively and rein in those who talk too much.

Groups don't make good decisions automatically. But a leader who works to establish healthy norms, such as controversy, and who takes action when destructive patterns set in, can help enormously.

EPILOGUE

HOW DID WE DO?

Evaluation Questions

ONE LAST KIND OF QUESTION that leaders consistently prize is the evaluation question. In *How to Lead Small Groups*, Dr. Neal McBride writes wisely and thoroughly about helping a group to evaluate itself.[1] Here I'd like to suggest two simple questions that you can use in five minutes at the end of every group meeting:

- What went well?
- What could we improve?

When people believe they can truly say what they think in response to these questions, they never need to leave the meeting seething about something that annoyed them. They also get a chance to celebrate a fruitful study, a deep time of personal sharing, or an effective process of decision-making. The leader gets instant feedback and can adjust the next meeting accordingly. Group members get instant feedback, so the leader doesn't carry the whole load of admonishing those who talk too much or take the group off on tangents.

Like most great questions, these two are simple, but they open doors to things the group probably won't learn any other way. That's the power of a truly great question.

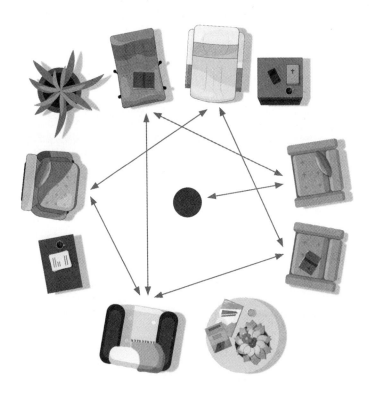

NOTES

CHAPTER 2: TELLING OUR STORIES

1. Roberta Hestenes, *Turning Committees into Communities: A Surprisingly Effective Means for Preventing Worker Burnout, While Boosting Morale at the Same Time* (Colorado Springs, CO: NavPress, 1991), 28.
2. For detailed instructions about giving your spiritual autobiography in a group setting, see Richard Peace, *Spiritual Storytelling: Discovering and Sharing Your Spiritual Autobiography* (Colorado Springs, CO: NavPress, 1996).

CHAPTER 4: A MATTER OF INTERPRETATION

1. Lewis Carroll, *The Annotated Alice: The Definitive Edition* (New York: W. W. Norton & Company, 2000), 213.

CHAPTER 7: SO WHAT?

1. *Relationships: Resolving Conflict and Building Community*, Foundations for Christian Living Series (Colorado Springs, CO: NavPress, 1997), 87.

CHAPTER 8: DECISIONS, DECISIONS

1. Roger von Oech, *A Kick in the Seat of the Pants* (New York: HarperCollins, 1986), 30.
2. David W. Johnson and Frank P. Johnson, *Joining Together: Group Theory and Group Skills* (Englewood Cliffs, NJ: Prentice Hall, 1987), 83.
3. Johnson and Johnson, 102.
4. Johnson and Johnson, 224.

EPILOGUE: HOW DID WE DO?

1. Neal F. McBride, *How to Lead Small Groups* (Colorado Springs, CO: NavPress, 1990), 117–139.

ABOUT THE AUTHOR

KAREN LEE-THORP is the author of more than seventy small-group study guides and Bible studies, from the LifeChange series to the Daniel Plan to video discussion guides with Lysa TerKeurst and Ann Voskamp. She also leads small groups at her local church. Her books include *Why Beauty Matters*, *The Story of Stories*, and *A Compact Guide to the Christian Life*. She holds a BA in history from Yale University.

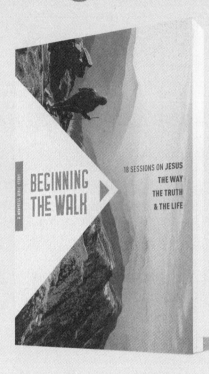

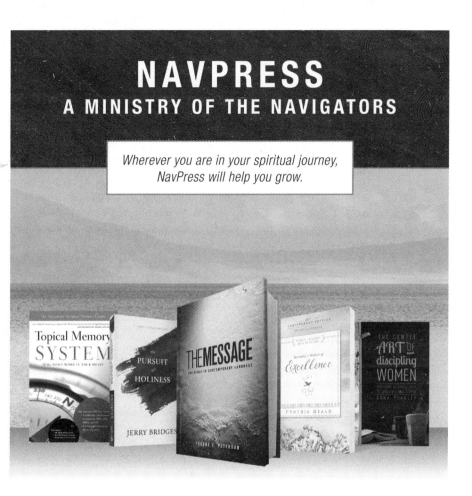

THE NAVIGATORS® STORY

THANK YOU for picking up this NavPress book! I hope it has been a blessing to you.

NavPress is a ministry of The Navigators. The Navigators began in the 1930s, when a young California lumberyard worker named Dawson Trotman was impacted by basic discipleship principles and felt called to teach those principles to others. He saw this mission as an echo of 2 Timothy 2:2: "And the things you have heard me say in the presence of many witnesses entrust to reliable people who will also be qualified to teach others" (NIV).

In 1933, Trotman and his friends began discipling members of the US Navy. By the end of World War II, thousands of men on ships and bases around the world were learning the principles of spiritual multiplication by the intentional, person-to-person teaching of God's Word.

After World War II, The Navigators expanded its relational ministry to include college campuses; local churches; the Glen Eyrie Conference Center and Eagle Lake Camps in Colorado Springs, Colorado; and neighborhood and citywide initiatives across the country and around the world.

Today, with more than 2,600 US staff members—and local ministries in more than 100 countries—The Navigators continues the transformational process of making disciples who make more disciples, advancing the Kingdom of God in a world that desperately needs the hope and salvation of Jesus Christ and the encouragement to grow deeper in relationship with Him.

NAVPRESS was created in 1975 to advance the calling of The Navigators by bringing biblically rooted and culturally relevant products to people who want to know and love Christ more deeply. In January 2014, NavPress entered an alliance with Tyndale House Publishers to strengthen and better position our rich content for the future. Through *THE MESSAGE* Bible and other resources, NavPress seeks to bring positive spiritual movement to people's lives.

If you're interested in learning more or becoming involved with The Navigators, go to www.navigators.org. For more discipleship content from The Navigators and NavPress authors, visit www.thedisciplemaker.org. May God bless you in your walk with Him!

Sincerely,

DON PAPE
VP/PUBLISHER, NAVPRESS

www.navpress.com

CP1308